Jesus
Friend of Children

Arthur S. Maxwell

REVIEW AND HERALD® PUBLISHING ASSOCIATION
Washington, DC 20039-0555
Hagerstown, MD 21740

PRINTED IN U.S.A.

ISBN 0-8280-0464-1

CONTENTS

The Miracle of Bethlehem

EVERY road in Palestine was crowded. Not in a long while had there been so much traffic. Families living in the south were moving north, and others living in the north were going south. Clouds of dust rose from the rough dirt roads as people in oxcarts, on horseback, on donkeyback, and on foot went by on their various ways.

The reason for all the disturbance was that there had gone out a decree from Caesar Augustus "that all the world should be taxed." "Enrolled" is the word in the margin of Luke 2:1. The emperor of Rome wanted money, and he wanted also to find out how many people there were in his empire. So everyone had to return to his home town to be taxed and counted. If you belonged to Jerusalem and were living in Jericho, you had to go back to Jerusalem. If you had been born, say, in Capernaum, and were living in Joppa, you had to take the long, dusty trip back to Capernaum, or perhaps get into trouble with the Roman soldiers, who were everywhere. So

"all went to be taxed, every one into his own city." Verse 3.

If you had been standing somewhere on the main north-south highway at that time—say a mile or so out of Jerusalem—you would have seen a sight to make your heart ache. Riding on a donkey was a girl, young and beautiful, but very tired. The shawl about her face was dusty, as was all her clothing. You could see by the weary look on her face that she longed for a place where she could stop and rest. But there could be no stopping, for the hour was late, and they had to reach Bethlehem before nightfall. With so many people traveling, the inn might be full and then what would happen? There was the Baby to think of. He might be born that very night. And He was the most important Baby in the world!

Joseph, walking at her side, was worried too. He was afraid the gates of Bethlehem might be closed before they got there. He wanted to hurry, but he dared not. There was nothing he could do but trudge on patiently, speaking a word of courage to Mary now and then.

Though the two tired travelers did not realize it, angels were watching them every step of the way. And if angels ever get anxious, they were worried too. They were thinking of the motion of the donkey, the ruts in the road, and the constant danger of a fall. If that Baby should be born too soon! That was unthinkable. He just *had* to be born in Bethlehem! So they watched and hoped and hovered over the humble little procession as it moved, oh, so slowly, on its weary way.

They had passed Jerusalem now. Only six miles more! How long seemed the last lap of the journey!

Presently, in the gathering dusk they could see a group of

flat-topped houses built on a hillside, and Joseph no doubt cried out with relief, "There it is! That's Bethlehem! Just a little farther. Soon we'll be at the inn, and then you can rest all night in comfort."

New strength came to both of them as they moved on up the hill. They were so happy that the long, tedious journey was almost over that they scarcely noticed all the other people hurrying past them with the same thought in mind of finding a place to stay before nightfall.

Darkness was upon them, and little oil lamps were burning in many a house when, at long last, they entered the village and made their way toward the inn. Now they were delayed by the people, the animals, and the carts that thronged the narrow streets. Finally, however, they reached the inn and knocked on the door.

The innkeeper appeared. "Sorry, no vacancy. Every room was booked long ago."

"But the girl and the Baby! The Baby might be born any time now. Surely you could find a corner for them somewhere?"

"Sorry, but there isn't a place anywhere—at least not in the inn."

"Well, is there anywhere else?"

"Every place in town is crowded."

"But, sir, the Baby——"

"Well, there's the stable. You may take shelter there if you care to."

The stable! They had so hoped for a bed in the inn. All the way Mary had been wondering just where "the Son of the

Highest" might be born. Perhaps
in the inn. Perhaps in somebody's
home. But never in a stable. Not there, of all
places. But a stable it had to be.

As the door creaked on its hinges, they caught the first
smell of the cows and the dung. What a place to sleep! What
a place for a baby to be born! What a place for the Messiah to
appear!

Of course, if the innkeeper had known what Mary knew,
he would have made room for her somewhere. Certainly he
would not have sent her to the stable. What a blessing he lost
that night! If he had given up his own room for the Saviour's
birth it would have been a source of joy and holy pride to him
the rest of his life. He would have been able to talk about it to
his friends and his customers, his children and his grandchil-
dren. Thousands upon thousands would have trekked to his
door just to see the place and hear his story. In his heart and

in his pocketbook he would have been blessed beyond all imagining. By failing to be kind to a poor, needy girl he missed the greatest opportunity of his life. Perhaps he is one of those who will one day hear Jesus say, "Inasmuch as ye did it not to one of the least of these, ye did it not to Me." Matthew 25:45.

What a lesson to us to be kind to everyone in need! We can never be quite sure who the needy one is, or what the consequences of our good deed may be.

Now Joseph is lighting the wick of a little oil lamp. Its feeble, flickering rays reveal what a dank, gloomy place the stable is, with its low roof, its rough beams, and its mud-and-straw-covered floor. Cows turn their heads and moo as the strangers enter. Rats scurry away to their holes.

Where to go? Down at the end there is an empty stall, and they go there. Joseph gathers straw to make a bed for Mary. But she is thinking only of the Baby. Where shall she put the Baby when He comes?

She spies the manger, half filled with hay for the cows to eat. The very thing! Not very beautiful, but soft and cozy, and at least He will be safe in it. He couldn't fall out.

Sinking gently upon the straw to rest, and looking out in the shadows all about her, Mary may well have thought to herself, Too bad that He should have to be born here! What was it that the angel had said? How well she remembered! "The Holy Ghost shall come upon thee, and the power of the Highest shall overshadow thee: therefore also that holy thing which shall be born of thee shall be called the Son of God."

The Son of God! To be born in a stable!

This Day a Saviour

SUPPOSE you had been living in Bethlehem the night that Jesus was born—"the night before Christmas," the first Christmas—wouldn't that have been wonderful! Of course, you might have been so tired that night you would have slept through everything that happened. Most people did.

But suppose some children, just one or two maybe, *were* awake that night. What did they see? What did they hear?

Ben and his little sister Ruth loved to sleep on the roof of their flat-topped house—that is, when father and mother gave them permission to do so. They liked to feel the cool breeze blowing over them and to lie on their backs, looking up into the sky, trying to count the stars.

This night was just like any other night except that there was something new to talk about. There was Caesar's decree about the taxing that had brought so many people to town.

"I never saw so many people in all my life," said Ben.

"Nor I," said Ruth. "Nor so many horses and oxen. The place is full of them. I wonder how long everybody will stay?"

"Only till the taxing is over, I suppose."

There was silence for a while.

"I've been wondering and wondering," said Ben.

"Wondering what?" asked Ruth. "About how long the people will stay?"

"No, no," said Ben. "Not that. But about what father has been telling us lately. You know, about the Messiah's coming. He says that the old prophecies must be fulfilled soon."

"Isn't it true that He is to come to Bethlehem?"

"Yes," said Ben. "He's coming to our town. The prophet Micah says so. I wonder when."

"Won't it be marvelous!" murmured Ruth, lying back on her bed of rushes. "Aren't we lucky that He's coming here!"

"I should say we are," said Ben. "I hope we don't miss Him. Let's go to sleep."

There was a pause.

"Ben! Look up there in the sky!"

"What at?"

"Look, look! That light! What can it be?"

"Oh my!" cried Ben. "Whatever is it? And it's almost over-head! Now it's coming low. It's right over the old inn. No, it isn't. It's over the stable behind the inn. I wonder what's hap-

pening? Let's go see! Quietly! Careful! Everybody's asleep."

Silently they slipped downstairs, across the road, and over toward the inn. Then they stopped, for the light now seemed to be outside the village.

"Look over there!" cried Ben. "Is it a fire?"

"Let's go see!" cried Ruth.

They ran on through the empty streets, then out across the fields to the place where shepherds brought their sheep at night for safety. The shepherds were standing in a group gazing at a beautiful being standing close beside them.

Could this be the promised Messiah everybody was expecting? No, not the Messiah, but an angel; and he was saying, "Fear not: for, behold, I bring you good tidings of great joy, which shall be to all people. For unto you is born this day in the city of David a Saviour, which is Christ the Lord." Luke 2:9-11.

Ben squeezed Ruth's hand.

"Did you hear that?" he whispered. "This is the night! Messiah has come! And He has come to Bethlehem!"

"S-sh!" whispered Ruth, entranced. "Listen! The beautiful angel is speaking again."

"And this shall be a sign unto you," said the angel. "Ye shall find the Babe wrapped in swaddling clothes, lying in a manger."

"Swaddling clothes!" whispered Ruth. "Then the Babe is just born. They only put newborn babies in swaddling clothes. I wonder where He is?"

Both were hushed to silence by what happened next; for "suddenly there was with the angel a multitude of the heavenly host praising God, and saying, Glory to God in the highest, and on earth peace, good will toward men." Verses 13, 14.

All heaven seemed flooded with light. Indeed, everywhere it was light as day. They could see the rugged mountains, the awestruck shepherds, the trembling sheep, and the white-walled houses and synagogues of Bethlehem. But what gripped them most was the vision of the angels. It was wonderful beyond words. So many angels! All of them singing as though their very lives depended on it, as though they had waited for ages and ages to sing this song.

"Glory to God! Glory to God! Glory to God in the highest!" The majestic music seemed to roll around the world and out toward the stars to the farthest reaches of infinite space. "Glory to God in the highest!"

Then in softer cadences, "On earth peace, good will toward men." How tenderly and hopefully they sang these closing words of their hymn of praise! It was as if they longed to see men everywhere welcome the Saviour with open arms and open hearts, and make the Son of God the Lord of their lives. Then, they knew, there would be peace on earth and good will among men.

As suddenly as they had come, the angels vanished. Darkness settled again over the hills and fields.

"And it came to pass, as the angels were gone away from them into heaven, the shepherds said one to another, Let us now go even unto Bethlehem, and see this thing which is come to pass, which the Lord hath made known unto us. And they came with haste." Verses 15, 16.

What haste! Can't you see them running as fast as their old legs would carry them, stumbling over holes and rocks and

briers, but getting up and hurrying on, bursting with the great news they had heard? And I like to think that maybe there were a couple of children there—for there are always some children about when something special is happening—running along behind, eager to see the wonderful Baby for which all Israel had been waiting so long.

In through the gates they clattered, down the cobbled streets. "Anybody know if a baby has been born in town to-night?" "Yes, down there, in the stable behind the inn."

It is still dark, but there is a light in the stable, and listen!

There is a faint cry of a tiny baby inside! This, then, must be the place!

One of the shepherds opens the old door. It creaks back on its hinges. They all step in. At first they see only the cattle in the stalls. Then, at the farther end, they make out a man standing, and a young woman resting on a pile of straw. Beside her, in the manger, is a baby. Obviously newborn, it is wrapped in swaddling clothes, just as the angel said.

Surely this *must* be the Saviour, the Messiah, Christ the Lord!

Reverently, but excitedly, the shepherds file down through the barn. Joseph and Mary look up startled, wondering what these strange men might want. Had they come to turn them out of the stable? No, indeed. They had come with news. Great news. One of them begins to explain. He tells how they were all there in the fields, just outside the village, keeping watch as usual over their flocks by night. Then how, of a sudden, an angel appeared and told them that this was the very night Messiah was to be born, and how they would find Him lying in a manger.

Mary's eyes glow. So she had not been mistaken! God had not forgotten her! He knew that she couldn't get into the inn that night. He knew His Son had had to be born in a stable and cradled in a manger. How comforting! God was watching over them, even though everything had seemed to go wrong. And if the angels had appeared to these shepherds, how near must they be to her!

Over and over the shepherds tell their story, with one or another breaking in every now and then to add some fresh detail about what happened on the hillside. And all the while they keep looking at the Babe, remarking on His beauty and loveliness. Then, as it dawns upon them ever more clearly that this is the Child of promise and prophecy, the long-looked-for Messiah, the Son of the living God, they kneel before Him in adoration.

By and by the shepherds leave. A new day is dawning—a new day for Bethlehem and for the world. People are waking up and getting breakfast. Some are already out of doors tending their animals. Imagine their amazement as they see the shepherds, whom they supposed to be out in the fields minding their sheep, "glorifying and praising God" in the main street of the village—stopping passers-by and telling them in excited voices of all the marvelous things they had seen and heard that night.

"You mean you saw angels? Angels here in Bethlehem?"

"Yes, indeed, a multitude of the heavenly host, praising God and saying——"

"Impossible!"

"But we did. And they said Messiah was born."

"Messiah born here last night! Oh, no. That couldn't be."

"Yes indeed. It's true! He's in the stable over there behind the inn."

"And all they that heard it wondered at those things which were told them by the shepherds."

The whole town was stunned.

Some believed their story, and some did not. Some went to the stable to see the Child. Some didn't bother to go. They let the greatest event of the ages go right past them without a thought. They busied themselves with their daily chores—washing dishes, cleaning house, feeding animals, making money—while the very One they said they wanted so much was right in their midst. How careful we need to be lest we get so burdened with cares that we do not realize when Jesus is near!

Of those who went to the stable that morning, some saw just another baby, and some saw God. It has been that way ever since. It is that way still. As you look at Him today, whom do *you* see?

Dangerous Days

NEWS about the Baby in the stable, and the shepherds' story of the angels they had seen, gave Bethlehem something to talk about for a day or two; but with all the rush and bother and business connected with the taxing, most people soon forgot all about it.

So there were no bands playing and no procession when Mary took her little Son to the Temple in Jerusalem to present Him to the Lord. Nobody in the jostling crowd pointed to her and said, "There is the mother of the Messiah!" or "That Baby she is carrying in her arms is the Son of God." Nobody, that is, until they came into the Temple. Then it was that old Simeon, to whom the Holy Spirit had spoken, saying that "he should not see death, before he had seen the Lord's Christ," suddenly recognized the Child. What a thrill of happiness surged through his dear old heart!

"Then took he Him up in his arms, and blessed God, and said, Lord, now lettest Thou Thy servant depart in peace, ac-

As Mary looked upon this lovely Babe in her arms, and pondered the far-reaching prophecy of Simeon, she was full of grateful joy and hope that here at last was Israel's Deliverer.

cording to Thy word: for mine eyes have seen Thy salvation, which Thou hast prepared before the face of all people; a light to lighten the Gentiles, and the glory of Thy people Israel."

Anna came in at that moment, and, beaming with joy as she looked at the Baby, "gave thanks likewise unto the Lord."

The service over, Mary and Joseph returned quietly to Bethlehem, marveling at all that had happened that day and "at those things which were spoken of Him."

Much greater excitement came to Jerusalem with the arrival of the Wise Men from the East. As they rode in on their camels through the city gate, everybody recognized them at once as men of wealth and position. Their fine clothes and stately appearance told that they were not of the common people. But the greatest interest was aroused by the question which they kept asking, "Where is He that is born King of the Jews? for we have seen His star in the east, and are come to worship Him." Matthew 2:2.

This set everybody talking. Some who had mocked at the story told by the poor shepherds were thrilled as these rich

strangers from the East spoke of following a star to find the King of the Jews. Others asked, "How could the King of the Jews be just born? The only king we know is Herod."

Soon all Jerusalem was agitated. The subject was even discussed in Herod's palace. When the king heard of it he became worried. Had a child really been born who would one day take his place as king of Israel? He sent for the chief priests and "demanded of them where Christ should be born." As king of the Jews he should have known without asking, but he had been too busy or too careless to find out.

"In Bethlehem of Judaea," replied the priests, quoting the prophecy of Micah 5:2.

So! thought Herod. Then I must find out if a child has been born in Bethlehem who might possibly become king. If so, I shall know what to do with him.

But how to find out? Possibly these Wise Men from the East would know. He sent for them and listened to their story. Particularly was he interested in the star which they said they had seen. The Bible says he "enquired of them diligently what time the star appeared." No doubt this was to find out how old the child might be.

Then he sent the Wise Men on to Bethlehem, saying, "Go and search diligently for the young child; and when ye have found Him, bring me word again, that I may come and worship Him also."

The old rascal! He had no thought of worshiping Jesus. He was planning to kill Him. But it sounded well, and the Wise Men no doubt thought what a good, kind king he was.

As they left the city gates, lo, there in the sky they saw the star again. Why they had lost sight of it, nobody knows. But whatever the reason, the star was there now, ready to guide them again.

And "when they saw the star, they rejoiced with exceeding great joy." Now they would keep their eyes fixed on it, no matter where it should lead them.

It did not take them far. Only six miles. Then it stopped, seeming to hover over a house in the village. Through the dark streets they hurried toward it, and knocked on the door.

Imagine the astonishment on Joseph's face as he opened the door and saw the Wise Men standing there in their rich robes! How he must have wondered who they were and why they had come! A moment later they were looking eagerly toward Mary and the Child they had come so far to see.

The Bible says, "When they were come into the house, they saw the young child with Mary His mother, and fell down, and worshipped Him."

As they rose from their knees they took packages from the folds of their long cloaks and unwrapped them. Mary's eyes opened in astonishment.

Gold! Jewels! Priceless treasures! To poor people like herself and Joseph, it was a fortune. She did not realize then that God had sent all this wealth to provide for the long journey they would soon have to take into Egypt.

There was frankincense and myrrh too—rich offerings usually reserved for princes, kings, and gods. Mary understood. It fitted in with all that the angel had said to her, and the shepherds, and Simeon and Anna in the Temple.

Having presented their gifts, the Wise Men prepared to leave and return to Jerusalem. They were eager to tell the king of their good fortune in finding the Child they had sought so long. But that night God warned them in a dream that they should not return to Herod. At once they saw through the king's wicked plan, and "they departed into their own country another way." Matthew 2:12.

As a result of the visit of the Wise Men, Jesus was, of course, in great danger. In Jerusalem, Herod waited for them to return and report the result of their search. How long he waited we do not know, but it could not have been more than a few days at most. Then, when they did not come, and he was told that they had disappeared, he was furious. His pride was hurt. He thought he had deceived *them,* and now, lo, they had deceived *him!* Now he would never know for sure about that Child they were seeking. Did they find Him, or not? Had a king been born in Bethlehem?

If Herod had not been so angry, he could have found out easily enough. Surely somebody in Bethlehem must have known about the visit of the Wise Men and just which house they had visited. But rage always makes people blind and foolish.

So, partly in anger because his wicked plan had failed, and partly to make sure that no king would come out of Bethlehem if he could help it, he ordered his soldiers to go to the village and kill every child "from two years old and under." That, he thought, would settle the matter.

But it didn't. God knew his thoughts, and planned a rescue. Even as Herod was giving his cruel order to his soldiers, the angel of the Lord appeared to Joseph in a dream, saying, "Arise, and take the young child and His mother, and flee into Egypt, and be thou there until I bring thee word: for Herod will seek the young child to destroy Him."

Joseph now saw the peril they were all in. Of course, if Herod should hear that the Wise Men had offered Jesus frankincense and myrrh, he would be very jealous. Perhaps his soldiers were on their way at this very moment. They must leave at once.

Mary was awakened. Together they packed their few belongings, not forgetting, of course, the precious treasures which the Wise Men had brought. These they hid where no prying eyes would find them. Then Joseph saddled the donkey, put Mary and the Child upon it, and set off.

Just in time! Hardly were they a safe distance from the village than Herod's soldiers arrived to do their murderous work. Perhaps upon the ears of the Baby Jesus—one day to be the comforter and burden bearer of His people—fell the cries of the poor little baby boys who died that night in Bethlehem.

The Best Boy Who Ever Lived

IT WAS not so very far from Bethlehem into Egypt, not more than a hundred miles at the most. Today you could cover that distance by car in two hours. At the pace a donkey travels, however, it may well have taken Joseph and Mary four or five days. How glad they must have been when at last they crossed the border into Egypt and felt safe from Herod's soldiers!

Just where they lived in Egypt no one knows, nor how long they stayed there. Probably Jesus was between two and three years old before they heard that Herod was dead and that it was now safe for them to return to their homeland.

At the time they left Bethlehem, the angel had said, "Be thou there until I bring thee word." So they had waited patiently for God's leading. At last the angel came. Once more he appeared to Joseph in a dream, saying, "Arise, and take the young child and His mother, and go into the land of Israel: for they are dead which sought the young child's life."

What a happy day that was! In Egypt, with the money the Wise Men had given them, they had been able to live in comfort; but it was not home. They knew they were strangers and foreigners there. Now they could go back and see their friends and loved ones again. So one day they left Egypt and came once more into the land of Israel.

Their first thought was to return to Bethlehem; but they were afraid to do that, for Herod's son, Archelaus, cruel as his father, was ruling there. So they journeyed north toward Nazareth, the place they had left at the time of the taxing by Caesar Augustus.

Back at last in their old home town, they started life anew, and lived peacefully there for many years. As for Jesus, we are told that "the child grew, and waxed strong in spirit, filled with wisdom: and the grace of God was upon Him." Luke 2:40.

These words suggest that He was a very good boy. And He was—the best boy who ever lived. It is a pity that we do not know more about His early days; how He helped Mary in the home and Joseph in his workshop. It must have been wonderful to have such a boy about the place, so kind, so thoughtful, so loving, so considerate of others.

The words "strong in spirit" would suggest that He was no

sissy. He had a mind of His own. He had opinions and a
will. Brave and fearless, He refused to go with the other
boys of the village when they were up to mischief. He was always ready to stand alone for right, even though it meant being
laughed at by His friends.

From His earliest days He studied the Bible with His
mother. Of course, they had only the Old Testament then, but
Jesus learned all its greatest passages by heart. He could recite
many of the psalms of David, the prophecies of Isaiah, and, of
course, the Ten Commandments.

Remembering what the angel Gabriel had said to her before her Baby was born, and all that had happened at Bethlehem at the time of His birth, Mary led Jesus to study especially
the chapters that mention the Messiah. Soon He knew where
to find them all. One day—we know not when—the Spirit of

God revealed to Him that they were all to be fulfilled by Him.

Every Friday evening the little family would kneel together to welcome the holy Sabbath. Every Saturday morning they would go to the synagogue for worship. It was their custom to do so (Luke 4:16). They never missed. The preacher could always be sure that Joseph, Mary, and that wonderful little Boy of theirs would be in their places in the house of God. What a privilege it must have been for the minister to preach to a Boy like that in church, so attentive and interested, always looking up with such keen, wide-open eyes!

Many times Joseph and Mary talked with Jesus about the yearly Passover services in Jerusalem. "Someday," they told Him, "when You are old enough, we will take You to see them."

Poor people, and poor people's children, did not get many treats those days, and a trip to Jerusalem must have seemed very wonderful to the son of a carpenter in Nazareth. No doubt

Jesus looked forward with great eagerness to the time when He would be twelve years of age and so could go to the big city.

At last, however, the longed-for day arrived, and the family set off on their journey. How interested Jesus must have been in everything and everybody—in the people who were thronging the roads to the holy city, in the things they talked about, in the animals on which they rode, but most of all in the great historical ceremony He was going to attend, and of which He had read so often in the books of Moses! All the way He asked questions about it. What would it be like? What did each part of the service mean?

The first sight of Jerusalem, with the Temple gleaming in the sunlight, must have brought a great thrill to His heart. Any boy of twelve would have been excited. Joyfully He entered the city gate and climbed the Temple steps. His sharp eyes took in everything—the priests offering a sacrifice, the dying

lamb, and the smoke of the altar fire spiraling up to heaven.

Mary had told Him much about all these things before, but now, as He saw them for Himself, they made a deep impression upon Him. If they pointed forward to the Messiah, then would Messiah have to die, Himself a sacrifice? Thus the mystery of His own mission gradually opened before Him.

There was a school attached to the Temple, and Jesus went in to see it. Here it was that He began asking questions of the priests, and they, amazed at His knowledge of the Scriptures, began asking questions of Him. So interested did they become that they did not want the Boy to leave.

Hours slipped by, and meanwhile the people who had attended the Passover began to leave. Joseph and Mary went with them. Having learned to have perfect trust in their Son, and knowing that He would never do anything wrong, they went on their way without a worry, even though He was not with them. Jesus was always so trustworthy, so reliable. They supposed He was with friends and would catch up with them in a little while. But when several hours had passed and He did not appear, they began to fear that some harm might have come to Him. So they started back to the city, asking everyone they met, "Have you seen Jesus? Our little Boy, you know. He's just twelve. Can you tell us where He is?"

Some said they had seen Him during the Passover, but nobody knew where He was now. So Joseph and Mary went all the way back to Jerusalem, getting more and more anxious every minute.

Now where to go? In her heart Mary knew there was only

After the Passover services had come to an end Jesus slipped away from His parents and went to the Temple to reason with the rabbis. They marveled at His knowledge of the Scriptures.

one place Jesus was likely to be. And it wasn't some place of amusement. It was the Temple.

So they made for the Temple.

"Is our Jesus here?" they asked.

Yes, He was there all right. Not just playing, as other boys of His age might have been, but "sitting in the midst of the doctors, both hearing them, and asking them questions." And the doctors seemed to be enjoying themselves most of all, for "all that heard Him were astonished at His understanding and answers." Never had they met a boy who knew the Scriptures so well and who understood their meaning so perfectly. And His questions! The wisest men there found them very hard to answer.

As Mary looked in on the scene she was amazed, as well she might have been. But she was so glad to find her Son that she forgot all about the learned doctors and ran right over to Him with outstretched arms.

"Son, why hast Thou thus dealt with us?" she said to Him in tender rebuke. "Behold, Thy father and I have sought Thee sorrowing."

Jesus was equally surprised to see His mother, and perhaps just a little sorry that this wonderful meeting with the doctors should have to come to an end.

"How is it that ye sought Me?" He asked. "Wist ye not that I must be about My Father's business?"

"My Father's business." That was a strange thing for a boy to say.

The doctors heard Him say it, and wondered what He meant. How could this man Joseph, they thought, a mere carpenter of Nazareth, have any business in the Temple? But Mary knew what He meant. Jesus was not thinking of Joseph. He was thinking of God. He believed that in learning more of the Scriptures, and storing up their wonderful truths in His mind, He was doing God's business, preparing Himself for what God would call Him to do when He was grown up.

This is still God's business today, for you and for me. Some people think that to spend time studying the Bible or going to church to hear someone preach the Word of God is wasting time. It isn't. It is the most important thing we can do. It is our Father's business, and in doing it we are helping to make ourselves strong and wise for the tasks that God will call us to do for Him in days to come.

Amid the friendly farewells of the doctors, Jesus left the Temple with Mary and Joseph. Then together they made their way back to Nazareth, where for many years more He lived with them and "was subject unto them." That is, He honored them and obeyed them, as all children should honor and obey their parents today.

Called to Service

SLOWLY the happy, carefree years in Nazareth passed away—the years of daily duties in the old home, of labor in the carpenter's shop, of Bible study and prayer with Mary and Joseph. Now the years of larger service were at hand.

One day news came to Jesus at Nazareth that His cousin John had begun to preach with great power down by the Jordan River. Thousands of people were flocking to hear him.

"He preaches like one of the ancient prophets," says one excited messenger. "He says he is 'the voice of one crying in the wilderness, Prepare ye the way of the Lord.' Some people are wondering whether he might be the promised Messiah, but he says, No, but He will appear soon. 'I indeed baptize you with water,' John says; 'but one mightier than I cometh, the latchet of whose shoes I am not worthy to unloose: He shall baptize you with the Holy Ghost and with fire.'"

"He's a powerful preacher and no doubt about it," reports another. "He's afraid of nobody. You should have heard

CALLED TO SERVICE

him talk to the Pharisees and Sadducees when they came to hear him. 'O generation of vipers,' he said to them, 'who hath warned you to flee from the wrath to come? Bring forth therefore fruits meet for repentance: and think not to say within yourselves, We have Abraham to our father: for I say unto you, that God is able of these stones to raise up children unto Abraham.' What a sermon was that! Israel has heard nothing like it since the days of Elijah."

Jesus was deeply moved by the reports that reached Him about His cousin, and at last He decided to go down to the Jordan and hear John Himself. In His heart He felt sure that the way John was stirring up the people and calling the whole nation to prepare for the appearance of the Messiah was all part of God's plan and a clear sign that His own great mission must soon begin.

Bidding farewell to His mother, to the old carpenter shop, and to everything around that was so familiar and dear to Him, He strode down the hill to the Jordan—and the new life He now must lead.

It was not hard to find the way to the place where John was preaching, for it seemed as though all the inhabitants of Jerusalem and Judea had left their homes and were headed in the same direction.

Jesus mingled with the crowd. Then, when John called for men and women to turn again to God and show their repentance by being baptized in the Jordan, Jesus went forward with the rest and humbly waited His turn. Scores of people were baptized. It must have been a wonderful sight. Presently

John came to where Jesus was standing. For a moment he did not know what to do. He knew that Jesus was the One about whom he was preaching—the Messiah for whom all were waiting. So he said, "I have need to be baptized of Thee, and comest Thou to me?"

Humbly Jesus answered, "Suffer it to be so now: for thus it becometh us to fulfil all righteousness."

If it was right for the people to be baptized, then Jesus wanted to be baptized too. Thus He would be an example for all who should afterward believe in Him. So John gently lowered Him into the waters of the Jordan and lifted Him up again. Then Jesus "went up straightway out of the water: and, lo, the heavens were opened unto Him, and He saw the Spirit of God descending like a dove, and lighting upon Him: and lo a voice from heaven, saying, This is My beloved Son, in whom I am well pleased." Matthew 3:16, 17.

What a moment was that! It marked the end of all the years of training and preparation that Jesus had had in Nazareth. He had been a dutiful son of His father and mother. He had been an example of kindness and purity to His brothers. He had mingled with His townsmen as a common carpenter, doing His work with efficiency and faithfulness. He was now to begin the great work for which God had sent Him into the world. Now He was indeed the Messiah, the Anointed One —anointed by the Holy Spirit and approved by His Father.

Was Jesus happy when He heard God say, "This is My beloved Son, in whom I am well pleased"? I think He must have been very, very happy for this evidence of God's approval.

How much these sweet words tell us of the character of Jesus! What a good boy He must have been! What a noble, straightforward youth! Day by day, week by week, month by month, year by year, God had been watching His growth and development. Angels had hovered near Him from Bethlehem to Nazareth, and now to Jordan. Never had they seen one failure, never a deed or a word of which they had felt ashamed. Never had Jesus disappointed them. He "was in all points tempted like as we are, yet without sin."

Now as God looked back upon the boyhood of Jesus, upon His youth and early manhood, He was justly proud of Him.

Gladly He recognized Him as His own. The very words "This is My beloved Son" suggest that He wanted everybody to know how very satisfied He was.

"In whom I am well pleased." What a beautiful commendation! Would you like your father to say this about you? I know you would. But *could* he say it? Could your mother? Could God?

God wants us all to live so like Jesus that He may be able to use these very words about us. Yes, about you and me. Let us ask Him now to help us to be so good and kind and true and faithful that someday we too may hear Him say, "This is My beloved son—My beloved daughter—in whom I am well pleased."

JESUS' MINISTRY

*J*esus began His ministry on earth. He began to teach about God's coming kingdom and the love God wanted to show every person on earth. He told how He had come to earth to bring salvation to all who would accept it. But He did more than just talk about love and salvation. He showed it in action. He would visit whole villages and heal every sick person in them. Those who were sad or lonely or discouraged He would comfort.

Men and women, boys and girls—all loved to be around Him. He made them feel loved and wanted. Children happily climbed into His lap. Adults told Him all about their problems. Problems and difficulties seemed to vanish when He talked to them.

People began to love Him so much that they thought it would be wonderful to be with Him forever. He told them that someday that would be possible. He would take all those who accepted His love to live with Him in heaven throughout all eternity. Jesus would have to go back to heaven, but He would return for them.

Until His second coming they would have to live special lives for Him, using all the special gifts and talents He had given them. He taught them how to use those gifts and talents. And He taught them what His second coming would be like.

Passport to Heaven

AFTER telling His disciples to be ever on the watch for His return and, in the meantime, to make the most of all the talents He had given them, Jesus drew back the curtain of the future once more and let them glimpse the wonderful scene when He will sit at last upon His throne of glory as King of kings and Lord of lords.

"When the Son of man comes in His glory," He said, "and all the angels with Him, then He will sit on His glorious throne. Before Him will be gathered all the nations, and He will separate them one from another, as a shepherd separates the sheep from the goats: and He will place the sheep at His right hand, but the goats at the left."

As the disciples pictured this happy day, their eyes sparkled with gladness. How they wanted their Master to be a king! How they longed to see His dream of a worldwide kingdom of love come true! How they hoped that they might have a part in it some day!

But what was this about sheep and goats? Who were the sheep and who were the goats? And how would Jesus separate them?

Eagerly they waited for the rest of the story. And Jesus said, "Then the King will say to those at his right hand, 'Come, O blessed of My Father, inherit the kingdom prepared for you from the foundation of the world: for I was hungry and you gave Me food, I was thirsty and you gave Me drink, I was a stranger and you welcomed Me, I was naked and you clothed Me, I was sick and you visited Me, I was in prison and you came to Me.'

"Then the righteous will answer Him, 'Lord, when did we see Thee hungry and feed Thee, or thirsty and give Thee drink? And when did we see Thee a stranger and welcome Thee, or naked and clothe Thee? And when did we see Thee sick or in prison and visit Thee?'

"And the King will answer them, Truly, I say unto you, as you did it to one of the least of these My brethren, you did it to Me."

These are the sheep. Christ's sheep. They stand at His right hand. They are the men and women, the boys and girls, who show kindness to others, whose hearts are filled with love and sympathy for the least of His brethren. They inherit His kingdom.

And the goats? They are the little, selfish people who never give a thought to other people's needs and sufferings.

To them Jesus will say, "I was hungry, and you gave Me no food, I was thirsty, and you gave Me no drink. I was

en the King will say to those at His right
d, 'Come, O blessed of My Father, inherit
kingdom prepared for you.'" And with
the faithful will enter the city of God.

a stranger, and you did not welcome Me, naked, and you did not clothe Me, sick and in prison, and you did not visit Me."

They will answer, "Lord, when did we see Thee hungry or thirsty or a stranger or naked or sick or in prison, and did not minister to Thee?"

And He will answer them, "Truly, I say to you, as you did it not to one of the least of these, you did it not for Me."

For these there will be no kingdom, no heaven, no eternal happiness. Instead they will share the punishment of the devil and his angels. Jesus said so Himself.

So it is love that makes the difference. It is love that separates those who are saved from those who are lost. It is love that decides whether we shall be among the sheep or the goats in the day of judgment.

Love is the passport to heaven. If we do not have it in our hearts—if we do not show it by gracious words and kindly

deeds, we shall never enter the kingdom of God. For His kingdom is a kingdom of love. It is made up of a people who love one another. And its King is the King of love.

And if love is so very important, maybe we should be looking around to see whether there is anyone who needs to be loved by us.

Think a moment. Is there somebody you know who is hungry, somebody whom you could feed? Maybe some poor little boy at school would be glad for a part of your lunch some day. Or a drink out of your nice new vacuum bottle.

And what about that new girl in your class, or the one who has just come to live next door? Are you being as friendly as you should? Have you said, "Welcome!" and meant it?

Maybe there's somebody you know who doesn't have money enough to buy clothes to keep himself warm. Could you share some of yours?

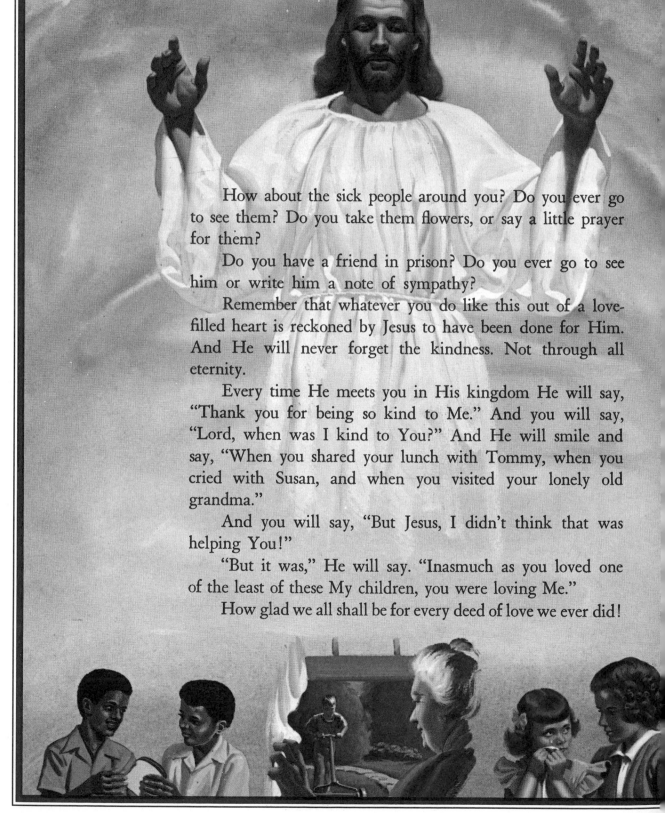

How about the sick people around you? Do you ever go to see them? Do you take them flowers, or say a little prayer for them?

Do you have a friend in prison? Do you ever go to see him or write him a note of sympathy?

Remember that whatever you do like this out of a love-filled heart is reckoned by Jesus to have been done for Him. And He will never forget the kindness. Not through all eternity.

Every time He meets you in His kingdom He will say, "Thank you for being so kind to Me." And you will say, "Lord, when was I kind to You?" And He will smile and say, "When you shared your lunch with Tommy, when you cried with Susan, and when you visited your lonely old grandma."

And you will say, "But Jesus, I didn't think that was helping You!"

"But it was," He will say. "Inasmuch as you loved one of the least of these My children, you were loving Me."

How glad we all shall be for every deed of love we ever did!

Falling Shadows

LITTLE more than three years had passed since Jesus had begun His ministry. Three short years. And yet already the shadows were gathering about Him. The dear old days with Mary at Nazareth seemed far, far away. So, too, the happy, peaceful hours with His disciples by the Sea of Galilee. Enemies were at work. People were criticizing His teachings, finding fault with the way He lived, ridiculing His humble birth, scoffing at His miracles.

The trouble was, of course, that Jesus had tried to change the lives of people who didn't want to be changed. He had sought to show them a better way of life, but they preferred their old ways. He had brought them light, but they chose darkness, because their deeds were evil.

Truly "the common people heard Him gladly." They loved Him for His beautiful teachings, and because He healed them of their diseases. But there were many others, like the priests and the Pharisees, whose lives were so different from the pure, humble, gentle life of Jesus that they hated Him. They hated Him because He was good. They hated Him because He was loved. They hated Him because He had a power they could not understand.

So they plotted to take His life. "Then assembled together the chief priests, and the scribes, and the elders of the people, unto the palace of the high priest, who was called Caiaphas, and consulted that they might take Jesus by subtilty, and kill Him." Matthew 26:3, 4.

It is terrible to think of all those religious leaders gathered together trying to think of some way to catch Jesus secretly and murder Him. But that is what they did.

Jesus knew about it, but He did not run away. It would have been easy for Him to have done so. He knew the lonely places on the mountains better than anyone else. And there was many a humble home where He could have hidden if He had wanted to.

But He did not hide. He had come for a great purpose, and He was willing to pay the price.

He knew from the book of Daniel that Messiah would have to die. Did not the prophecy say, "After threescore and two weeks shall Messiah be cut off, but not for Himself"? And what was it Isaiah had said? "Surely He hath borne our griefs, and carried our sorrows. . . .

He was wounded for our transgressions, He was bruised for our iniquities. . . . He is brought as a lamb to the slaughter."

Jesus remembered also the words which John the Baptist had said to Him at His baptism: "Behold the Lamb of God, which taketh away the sin of the world." John 1:29.

Every day lambs were slain by the priests in the Temple as a sacrifice for sin. All pointed to Him and the work that He must do.

So Jesus said to His disciples, "After two days is the feast of the passover, and the Son of man is betrayed to be crucified."

"To be crucified!" Surely Jesus could not mean that! What had He done to deserve so terrible a punishment? They could not believe it. They felt sure He would never let anything like that happen to Him. Why, it was only a couple of days ago that He had ridden into Jerusalem on a donkey with

all the children crying out, "Hosanna to the Son of David!" Surely He would not let Himself be put to death so soon after that. His work was only beginning!

But the shadows continued to fall. Thursday evening came—Passover night. Jesus and His disciples gathered round a table to celebrate it. Everybody was gloomy. Then when Jesus said that one of them should betray Him, "they were exceeding sorrowful, and began every one of them to say unto Him, Lord, is it I?"

He answered: "The Son of man goeth as it is written of Him: but woe unto that man by whom the Son of man is betrayed!" Soon after this Judas left. "And it was night." Night outside and night in all their hearts.

After they had eaten the Passover, they sang a hymn and walked out along the dark streets, through one of the city gates, to the Mount of Olives. But Jesus did not want to talk now; He wanted to pray. Coming to the Garden of Gethsemane, He told most of those who were with Him to rest while He went on with Peter, James, and John.

But they, too, were tired, and soon fell asleep, leaving Jesus alone. Then it was that He prayed that sad, sad prayer, "O My Father, if it be possible, let this cup pass from Me: nevertheless not as I will, but as Thou wilt." Three times He prayed, using the same words. He did not want to die.

He did not want to suffer all the shame and pain of crucifixion. He shrank from the cruel torture of it. Yet He was willing to bear it all if it was God's will.

By and by "there appeared an angel unto Him from heaven, strengthening Him." Luke 22:43. So the angels were watching still! Just as at Bethlehem, so now in Gethsemane. But how different was the scene! Then all was happiness and light; now, only darkness and sorrow.

At last Jesus heard distant shouting, and saw the light of many torches moving in the darkness as an angry mob surged up the hill to take Him. The end was near.

"Rise," He called to His sleeping disciples, "let us be going: behold, he is at hand that doth betray Me."

A moment more and they were surrounded. Then Judas came forward and kissed Jesus—the sign he had agreed upon with the priests. Jesus said to him, with great gentleness, "Friend, wherefore art *thou* come?"

Peter, seeing armed men about to seize Jesus, drew his

sword and struck off the ear of one of them. It was a brave deed, but useless. "Put up again thy sword into his place," Jesus said to him: "for all they that take the sword shall perish with the sword." Then He touched the bleeding ear and restored it as it was before.

"Thinkest thou that I cannot now pray to My Father," He said to Peter, "and He shall presently give Me more than twelve legions of angels? But how then shall the scriptures be fulfilled, that thus it must be?" Of course He could have called the angels to help Him! And how glad they would have been to come to His rescue and scatter that howling mob! But it could not be. The Scriptures had to be fulfilled.

"And they led Jesus away to the high priest." Down the Mount of Olives, up the slope to Jerusalem, in through the gate, and over to the palace. His hands bound, His disciples gone, Jesus walked on bravely but sadly to the fate that awaited Him in the city He had come to save.

How Jesus Died

IT WAS very late by now, but the high priest was waiting for Jesus. So were "all the chief priests and the elders and the scribes." There they sat with dark, angry looks on their faces. They had made up their minds He should not escape this time. But they had to charge Him with some crime before they could condemn Him to death. And they couldn't find any. He had not done anything wrong.

True, "witnesses" came forward to accuse Jesus, but as they did not tell the truth they kept contradicting one another. As they did so, the high priest became more and more angry. Presently, seeing that his whole plan to kill Jesus might fail if things went on like this, he turned on Jesus Himself and cried, "Answerest Thou nothing?"

Jesus kept silent. There was no need for Him to reply to false charges.

Then the high priest, white with anger, blurted out, "Art Thou the Christ, the Son of the Blessed?"

"I am," Jesus answered: "and ye shall see the Son of man sitting on the right hand of power, and coming in the clouds of heaven." Mark 14:61, 62.

This was too much for the high priest. Tearing his robe in fury, he cried to the whole assembly, "What need we any further witnesses? Ye have heard the blasphemy: what think ye?"

"Death!" they cried angrily. "Put Him to death!"

But they could not kill Him themselves. Only the Roman governor could do that. So they had to wait till daylight. Then, "very early" Friday morning, they hurried Jesus over to Pilate's judgment hall. Everybody went—"the whole multitude," all shouting their hatred of Jesus.

How tired the Saviour must have been! Up all night with that angry, jeering throng. Slapped, beaten, spat upon, He was now dragged and shoved toward the judgment hall.

Because it was Passover time the Jews would not go into the hall themselves, so Jesus found Himself alone with Pilate. He was glad for that. He always liked to be alone with people so that He could speak to their hearts. He had been alone with Nicodemus, with the poor woman at the well, and now, in His last moments, with the Roman governor himself.

"Art thou the King of the Jews?" asked Pilate.

"Thou sayest," said Jesus. But lest the governor should misunderstand and think He was just a common rebel against the power of Rome, He added, "My kingdom is not of this world: if My kingdom were of this world, then would My servants fight, that I should not be delivered to the Jews: but now is My kingdom not from hence."

This was hard for a man like Pilate to understand. All the kings he had ever heard of fought for their kingdoms.

"Art Thou a king then?" he asked, puzzled.

"Yes," said Jesus. "To this end was I born, and for this cause came I into the world, that I should bear witness unto the truth."

"What is truth?" asked Pilate.

This was the governor's great chance to accept Jesus. But he did not take it. He was afraid. Hearing the shouting outside, he went out to the yelling mob.

"I find in Him no fault at all," he said.

At this the shouting grew louder. Pilate saw that these people were in a frenzy of rage and hatred.

Seeking a way out, he sent Jesus to Herod, ruler of Galilee, who happened to be in the city for the Passover. But Herod, after making fun of Jesus and putting a royal robe on Him, sent Him back to Pilate.

Again Pilate tried to save

Jesus. "I will . . . chastise Him, and release Him," he said.

"No!" shouted the mob. "Away with this Man, and release unto us Barabbas."

So they chose Barabbas—a murderer—rather than the Son of God.

"What then shall I do with Jesus?" Pilate asked.

"Crucify Him!" they yelled.

"Why, what evil hath He done?" said Pilate.

For answer they cried yet louder, "Crucify Him!"

At last Pilate gave way. First, he took water and washed his hands before the crowd, saying, "I am innocent of the blood of this just person: see ye to it." But no water could ever wash away his guilt. He could have saved Jesus, but he didn't.

Then the order was given that Jesus should be crucified, and the soldiers led Him away. In their common hall they treated Him so cruelly that when the time came for Him to be taken to the place of crucifixion He was half dead already. Having been scourged with a whip, and having had a crown of sharp thorns pressed down upon His head, He was so faint that He could scarcely stand.

Too weak to carry the great wooden cross that was laid on His shoulder, Jesus fell beneath it, and the soldiers looked for someone else to bear it for Him. Catching sight of a man called Simon who had come to Jerusalem from Cyrene in North Africa, they compelled him to carry the cross.

This man Simon, the Bible says, was "the father of Alexander and Rufus," and I have often wondered why those two boys are mentioned. Could it be because they were so proud that their dad carried the cross for Jesus? Surely they must have talked about it the rest of their days. It was something to be proud of too.

Slowly the sad procession wended its way to Calvary. "And there followed Him a great company of people, and of women, which also bewailed and lamented Him." Luke 23:27. Many who had heard Jesus preach were there, and many whom He had healed. There were children, too, some of the very ones who had cried "Hosanna to the Son of David!" only a few days before. They looked on with sad, frightened eyes.

At last the procession stopped at the place of execution. And there they crucified Him.

Laying Jesus on the cross, the soldiers drove nails through His hands and feet. The pain of it must have been dreadful. But all Jesus said was, "Father, forgive them; for they know not what they do." The original words suggest that He kept on saying it. Over and over again, instead of cursing and swearing like the two thieves who were crucified with Him, He repeated the beautiful words, "Father, forgive them." Only the Son of God could ever have done that.

Then the cross was lifted and thrown into a hole in the ground. Again the pain must have been terrible, but Jesus whispered, "Father, forgive them." No anger, only forgiveness.

So there at last He hung, between heaven and earth, with arms outstretched in suffering love for all the world to see. It was as though, in His last dying moments, He was saying, "Look unto Me, and be ye saved, all the ends of the earth." Isaiah 45:22.

Over His head was a sign saying, "This is Jesus the King of the Jews." Though put there in jest, how true it was—their King and our King, the Great Teacher of Nazareth, the Great Healer of Galilee, the Great Friend of little children—so kind, so wise, so gentle, so undeserving of all this cruelty!

Now, in the lovely words of Stainer's *Crucifixion:*

"Jesus is dying, in agony sore,
Jesus is suffering more and more,
Jesus is bowed with the weight of His woe,
Jesus is faint with each bitter throe,
Jesus is bearing it all in my stead,
Pity Incarnate for me has bled;
Wonder of wonders it ever must be,
Jesus, the Crucified, pleads for me."

By this time a great crowd had gathered round the cross.

"And sitting down they watched Him there" (Matthew 27: 36), even as the world has been watching Him ever since.

The soldiers watched as they gambled for His garments.

The priests watched, gloating over the victory they thought they had won, and shouting, "If Thou be the Son of God, come down from the cross."

The women who had followed Him watched, weeping.

People whom He had helped and healed watched, with bowed heads and sorrowful hearts.

There must have been children there too. Perhaps a little boy and girl holding hands, looking up at the cross with big, sad eyes, and tears rolling down their cheeks, as they whispered to each other, "Poor Jesus! He was so kind to us. He told us such lovely stories. Why did He have to die—like this?"

Why? Why? How often have we all asked why? The answer is given in the words of the lovely old hymn:

> "There is a green hill far away,
>   Without a city wall,
>   Where the dear Lord was crucified,
>   Who died to save us all.
>
> "We may not know, we cannot tell,
>   What pains He had to bear,
>   But we believe it was for us
>   He hung and suffered there.
>
> "He died that we might be forgiven,
>   He died to make us good,
>   That we might go at last to heaven,
>   Saved by His precious blood.

"There was no other good enough
     To pay the price of sin;
He only could unlock the gate
     Of heaven, and let us in.

"O dearly, dearly has He loved!
     And we must love Him too,
And trust in His redeeming blood,
     And try His works to do."
                    —C. F. ALEXANDER

The Boy Without a Name

CAN you imagine a baby coming to somebody's house and nobody having a name for it? I can't. Usually, just as soon as people know there's a baby coming, they begin choosing a name right away—one for a boy, and another in case it's a girl. To have no name ready at all would be very strange indeed. But it really happened once in the long ago.

When this particular baby boy turned up, his mother didn't know what to call him. Why, I don't know. Perhaps she just couldn't make up her mind whether he should be called John or Peter or Stephen or David. Maybe she read her list of names over and over again until she got into such a muddle she gave up in despair. Anyway, she gave up. And what do you suppose she did then? Well, believe it or not, she decided she would just call him Son of Papa.

What a funny name! It was. Yet, as you will see later, it was a name big with meaning, though the mother didn't know it then.

Hearing of the cruel death of Jesus, the children who loved Him must have been broken-hearted to find only an empty cross, the crown of thorns, and a few nails to tell the story.

Living in Bible times, this mother did not, of course, use our English words "son of papa," but the word *Bar,* meaning "son," and *Abba,* meaning "papa," or "father." So the little boy was called Barabbas.

Sad to say, he was not a good boy. He was always getting into trouble. I wouldn't be surprised if he was the ringleader of all the naughty boys in the district where he lived.

Whether Barabbas in his boyhood and early youth ever met John the Baptist or Jesus of Nazareth no one knows, though he lived at the same time and may have been among the crowds who went down to the Jordan to hear them preach. It is possible that he heard John say, "Bring forth therefore fruits worthy of repentance!" or Jesus plead with the people in His tender, gentle voice, "Come unto Me, all ye that labour and are heavy laden, and I will give you rest."

But if Barabbas ever heard these words, he did not heed them. He turned away from religion. His heart became hard and cruel. With a group of worldly young men like himself he started a riot and committed murder. For this he was arrested by the Roman soldiers and thrown into prison.

How grieved his mother must have been when she learned what had happened to the boy she had once called Son of Papa! And how worried Barabbas must have been, lying there in the dungeon, waiting in terror for his punishment!

Days passed—long, long days, and longer nights. Chained in his cell, Barabbas could hear carpenters at work in the courtyard, shaping his cross, and he knew the dreaded moment was close at hand.

Then one morning—very early—he was roused by the sound of a great commotion outside the prison. Through the window of his cell came loud, angry voices.

Louder and louder they became. It seemed as though thousands of people were shouting for vengeance on somebody. Who could it be? Who could have stirred up the whole city like this, and at such an hour of the morning?

And now, what was that?

"Barabbas! We want Barabbas!"

His name! They were shouting his name. He must die!

Suddenly he heard a rattling of keys. The guard! Perhaps they had come to hand him over to the angry crowd.

The cell door creaked open. Soldiers ordered him to rise and go with them. Tremblingly he obeyed.

Up the dark stairway, along stone corridors, marched the guard and their prisoner. Where could they be taking him? thought Barabbas. Presently, entering the governor's palace, he found himself face to face with none other than Pontius Pilate himself! And there, beyond him, was the crowd, that angry, seething crowd, still shouting, "Barabbas! Release to us Barabbas!"

Then his eyes rested upon Someone else—a sad and lonely figure standing near Pilate.

Surely I have seen that man before! he thought. Why, that is Jesus of Nazareth! That is the famous Teacher whom all the people love. What is He doing here? Surely He has committed no crime.

Then Pilate spoke to the crowd. "Whom will ye that I

release unto you? Barabbas, or Jesus which is called Christ?"

"Barabbas!" shrieked the crowd, "Barabbas!"

Pilate turned to the soldiers. "Let him go," he said. "Then released he Barabbas unto them."

Bounding down the steps, out into the crowd, Barabbas could hardly contain himself for joy. This was too wonderful for words. Instead of being crucified, as he had fully expected to be, he was free! Free! Pilate himself had released him!

By and by Barabbas noticed the crowd beginning to move away from the governor's palace. The people seemed to be moving toward the city gate, beyond which lay Golgotha, the place of execution. Rumor spread that three prisoners were to die there this day, all by crucifixion, that awful death which Barabbas had himself expected. He decided to follow the crowd.

Soon he came upon the sad procession of the condemned. Over the heads of the people in front of him he could see the crosses carried on the backs of the weary prisoners.

Who was the one in front, staggering under the weight of his cross? Why, surely, it was the same man whom he had seen that very morning in the presence of Pilate! It was the Preacher from Galilee—the kind, gentle Jesus—on His way to be crucified! Yes, and carrying the very cross that might have been his!

What happened to Barabbas after that we do not know. So far as the Bible story goes, he was lost in the crowd on that dreadful day. Perhaps his wicked heart may have been touched as he realized that Jesus had taken his place and was bearing that cross for him!

Did you ever stop to think how wonderful it is that it was a man called Bar-abbas whose cross Jesus carried? Being only "Son of Papa," he stands for every boy and every girl who ever lived, no matter how bad and naughty. If his name had been John or Peter or Stephen or David, some might have thought that Jesus bore the cross just for one person in particular. Then there would have been a chance that some poor, sinful soul might have felt left out. So in the providence of God the one whose place Jesus took, whose cross He bore to Calvary, was just Bar-abbas, "Son of Papa," the boy without a name.

From that moment on, everyone could feel sure that he was included in the glorious salvation which Jesus provided. Today, two thousand years later, every son and daughter of Adam, every boy and girl in every nation under heaven, may say with confidence, "He died for me."

When History Broke in Two

THAT day when Jesus died upon the cross was the most important in the history of this world. It was, in fact, the day when history broke in two.

Jesus had come from heaven to reveal the love of God to the world, to men and women, boys and girls, everywhere. He had come to tell them that "God so loved the world, that He gave His only begotten Son, that whosoever believeth in Him should not perish, but have everlasting life." John 3:16.

He had revealed this love by a thousand kindly deeds, and many a gracious word of sympathy, hope, and courage. He had fed the hungry, healed the sick, opened the eyes of the blind, made the lame to walk, even raised the dead to life. There was nothing else He could have done to let the people know that the God of heaven is a God of love, and that He cares for His earthly children night and day, in sunshine and in darkness, all the days of their lives, "even unto the end of the world."

Jesus had tried to tell everybody, too, that the love of God is so great that He is willing to forgive every sin, no matter how great, and to take into His kingdom all who truly repent of the wrong they have done. All He asks, said Jesus, is that one shall say in his heart, like the prodigal son, "I will arise and go to my father, and will say unto him, Father, I have sinned." Let any boy or girl say this, and mean it, and God will receive him gladly.

If anyone happened to say, "How can a perfectly just God overlook the breaking of His law?" Jesus replied, in effect, Don't worry; I am caring for that. Then He pointed to that beautiful passage of scripture in Isaiah 53, and applied it to Himself: "Surely He hath borne our griefs, and carried our sorrows. . . . He was wounded for our transgressions, He was bruised for our iniquities: the chastisement of our peace was upon Him; and with His stripes we are healed. All we like sheep have gone astray; we have turned every one to his own way; and the Lord hath laid on Him the iniquity of us all." Verses 4-6.

Now, to keep His promise, and to fulfill these words, He is dying on Calvary's cross. The Son of God, the Creator of the heavens and the earth, is giving His life for His one lost world. He who sat upon the throne of glory "from the years of eternity" is now hanging upon a cross. He whom angels once worshiped and adored is dying a criminal's death between two thieves!

No wonder there is "darkness over all the earth." For three awful hours, from noon till three o'clock, there has been no light from sun or moon or stars. In heaven angels veil their faces rather than look upon the dreadful scene.

Suddenly through the darkness comes a cry from the center cross, a cry as from one in great anguish. "My God, My God, why hast Thou forsaken Me?" Matthew 27:46. This is the moment of Jesus' greatest suffering. Not only is the torturing pain of crucifixion at its worst, but the whole awful weight of the sins of all mankind is pressing down upon His soul. He feels cut off from His Father's presence and companionship.

Now it is that

> "All the sins of man
> Since the world began
> Are laid, dear Lord, on Thee."

The words of that lovely hymn in Stainer's *Crucifixion* tell us:

> "Here the King of all the ages,
>   Throned in light ere worlds
>   could be,
> Robed in mortal flesh is dying,
>   Crucified by sin for me.
>
> "This—all human thought
>   surpassing—
>   This is earth's most awful hour,
> God has taken mortal weakness!
>   God has laid aside His power!"

And now another cry, a "loud voice," is heard from that center cross. "It is finished!" cries Jesus. "Father, into Thy hands I commend My spirit."

The struggle is over; the victory is won. Truly Jesus is dead, but in dying He has paid the price of man's redemption. He has opened the way into the kingdom of God for all who believe in Him. He has kept the promise He made to Adam and Eve in the Garden. He has made certain that the serpent's head shall be crushed, and that Eden, glorious Eden, shall be restored as the eternal home of His children.

So, though seemingly defeated by cruel enemies, Jesus has cleared the way for a complete and glorious triumph over all evil.

Suddenly, as Jesus becomes limp and lifeless on the cross, all nature is convulsed. The earth heaves to and fro in a

mighty quake. Great rocks split open. Lightning flashes and thunder roars. The very elements seem to be shouting their fury at the wicked deed that has been done. The crowd of sneering, jeering people about the foot of the cross melts away. Priests and rulers alike flee for their lives. Only the soldiers remain, with the centurion who says, "Truly this was the Son of God." Matthew 27:54.

In the midst of all these terrible happenings the veil of the Temple is suddenly "rent in twain from the top to the bottom."

This veil separated the holy place from the Holy of Holies—the two main apartments of the Temple in Jerusalem. And when that veil—no doubt by an eager angel's hand—was ripped from top to bottom, it told the Jewish people that their services and sacrifices were no longer needed. From this moment on they would be meaningless, for the one supreme sacrifice, toward which all others had pointed, had now been made.

Even as that Temple veil was torn in two that solemn Friday afternoon in the long ago, so the whole course of history was divided by what happened then. The crucifixion of Jesus was the Great Divide in the history of the world and of the universe. From then on everything was different, not only for the Jews, but for all mankind. Till then men had been looking forward to the coming of the Messiah to bear their griefs and carry their sorrows. Now they would forever look back to a Saviour who gave His life for the world.

By dying on Calvary, Jesus gave new meaning to His birth in Bethlehem, so that His whole life began to stand out as of supreme importance in the affairs of men and nations. People began to speak of B.C.—before Christ and A.D.—after Christ (meaning *Anno Domini,* the year of our Lord). And now everybody in all the world, Christians and non-Christians alike, uses these terms. Every history book is based on them.

Today we still look back to that turning point of time. And there we see a cross, with arms outstretched in loving invitation—one toward the past, the other toward the future —taking in everyone, every father and mother, every boy and girl, from Eden lost to Eden restored. And it stands on old Golgotha, where history broke in two.

> "When I survey the wondrous cross
>   On which the Prince of glory died,
> My richest gain I count but loss,
>   And pour contempt on all my pride.
>
> "Were the whole realm of nature mine,
>   That were a tribute far too small;
> Love so amazing, so divine,
>   Demands my life, my soul, my all."

The Saddest Sabbath

MANY tears were shed when Jesus died on Calvary's cross. Not all who watched His crucifixion had jeered and mocked at Him. Among the crowd there was more than one disciple heartbroken at the turn of events. "All His acquaintance, and the women that followed Him from Galilee, stood afar off, beholding these things." Luke 23:49.

Among those who cared most were "Mary Magdalene, and Mary the mother of James and Joses, and the mother of Zebedee's children." They had been very close to Jesus in all His work the past three years, and you can imagine how they must have felt when they saw Him crucified. They hoped against hope that even at the last minute Jesus would reveal His power and surprise everybody by coming down from the cross.

Sick with fear and disappointment, they waited helplessly, weeping their hearts out in sorrow. They saw noon be-

come dark as midnight, and for three hours they peered through the gloom at the three crosses on Golgotha's hill. They heard that last loud cry of their beloved Master; they felt the earth quake; they shuddered at the brilliant lightning and the rolling peals of thunder. Even now, they thought, amid these dreadful convulsions of nature, something might happen to raise their hopes anew. But no; it was all over. Jesus was dead. There was no hope now. There was nothing to do but go back to Jerusalem and weep.

And what would happen to His body? It would have to be taken from the cross before Sabbath; they knew that; but what would the Romans do with it? Oh, dreadful thought; would they cast it into a criminal's grave or leave it lying on the hillside for the crows and rats to devour? And what could a few poor women do about it?

Then word spread that a rich man who had been a secret disciple of Jesus had asked permission to take His body from the cross and bury it. It was Joseph of Arimathaea, "an honourable counsellor, which also waited for the kingdom of God." He had gone "boldly unto Pilate, and craved the body

of Jesus," and Pilate had granted his request.

It was the first good news the disciples had heard that day and I can almost hear those weeping women murmur, "God bless him! Brave man! Thank God for Joseph of Arimathaea!"

By and by Mary Magdalene and Mary the mother of Jesus, who had lingered by the cross after the others had left, saw Joseph and his friend Nicodemus — the one who came to Jesus by night—take the body from the cross, and carry it gently to "a sepulchre that was hewn in stone, wherein never man before was laid."

It was Joseph's own sepulcher, made for himself and his family. I have been in it, or one just like it. It is close by Golgotha. Inside you can still see how it was hewn out of the rock, and how it was left unfinished, brand new, when Jesus had need of it.

There was no burial service for Jesus, such as is held for the dead today. There was too little time between His death at three o'clock and the arrival of the Sabbath at sunset. Certainly there was no time to embalm His body. So Joseph and Nicodemus did the best they could, laying Him gently inside the tomb and rolling a stone across the door.

As for the two Marys, they "beheld the sepulchre, and how His body was laid. And they returned, and prepared spices and ointments; and rested the sabbath day according to the commandment." Luke 23:55, 56.

Why did they not go right on and embalm the body of Jesus then and there? Surely nothing could have been more important than that! Had not Jesus Himself said, "The sabbath was made for man, and not man for the sabbath"? Mark 2:27. Had He not also said, "It is lawful to do well on the sabbath days"? Matthew 12:12. Had He not healed the sick on the Sabbath, and done many other good deeds on that day? True, He had. But He had never told His disciples to break the Sabbath by doing unnecessary work during its sacred hours.

They were cruel hands of hate that nailed Jesus to the cross of Calvary, but the hands that took His body down and prepared it for burial were hands of tender love and sympathy.

After walking with Jesus for three and a half years, the disciples knew just how He felt about the fourth commandment and Sabbathkeeping. They had no question in their minds as to which day they should keep, or how they should keep it. So, because the embalming of the body of Jesus was not absolutely necessary just then, they left the task undone, returned to Jerusalem, and waited for the holy hours of the Sabbath to pass.

And what a sad, sad Sabbath that was! Surely it was the saddest Sabbath in all history. The disciples were in despair. Some had already started back to Galilee. The rest were hiding in and around Jerusalem, afraid that now Jesus was dead the priests and rulers would try to kill them also.

It was hard to believe that only a few days ago Jesus had ridden into Jerusalem at the head of a great procession of happy people, with some spreading palm branches before Him and children crying out, "Hosanna to the Son of David: Blessed is He that cometh in the name of the Lord." Matthew

21:9. But it was so, and everyone had thought that that was the moment when He would take over the government of Israel from the Romans and let Himself be crowned king. Eagerly, hopefully, they had waited for Him to reveal His power in some wonderful way, so that everyone would welcome Him as the long-hoped-for Messiah.

Now *this* had happened! In less than a week Jesus had been arrested, tried, condemned, crucified! So suddenly had it all taken place that some thought it must be just a bad, ugly dream. It was as though a great hole had opened in the earth and swallowed all their hopes. With Jesus gone, there was nothing left to hope for, nothing left to live for. What *would* they do without Him? What could they do?

They talked together of the beautiful life Jesus had lived among them, of the wise things He had said, of the kind deeds He had done, how gracious and gentlemanly He had been to everybody, even to His enemies. They wept anew at the very mention of His name.

On Sabbath morning word spread that the priests had learned where Jesus had been buried and had gone to Pilate urging that a guard of Roman soldiers be placed around the sepulcher.

The rumor was true. A delegation of priests and Pharisees had indeed gone to Pilate, saying, "Sir, we remember that that deceiver said, while He was yet alive, After three days I will rise again. Command therefore that the sepulchre

be made sure until the third day, lest His disciples come by night, and steal Him away, and say unto the people, He is risen from the dead: so the last error shall be worse than the first." Matthew 27:63, 64.

Pilate had granted their request, saying, "Ye have a watch: go your way, make it as sure as you can. So they went, and made the sepulchre sure, sealing the stone, and setting a watch."

As the news of this reached the disciples they plunged into deeper sorrow. Now what should they do? They had planned to go to the tomb after Sabbath to embalm the body of their Lord. Now even this might be denied them. Would the soldiers let them by?

Slowly the hours of that saddest Sabbath passed by. When at last sunset came again, it found them all still mourning for their Master. They could think of nothing else but that their beloved Jesus was dead and buried, and, worst of all, a hundred Roman soldiers were guarding His body and a Roman seal was upon His sepulcher.

Twin Sunrise

I DON'T suppose the disciples slept very much that Saturday night. They were too worried, too sorrowful, too afraid. Many of them no doubt spent the night getting ready to leave the city before the persecution they feared should break out. Others just went on talking of the terrible things that had happened that weekend, and of what they would have to do now Jesus had been taken from them.

But whether they slept, or lay awake, all were aroused and startled by another mighty earthquake in the early hours of the morning. Once more the earth trembled violently and all the houses shook.

What a day, what a night! they must have said.

Among those who slept little, if at all, were some of the women from Galilee, including those who had watched His burial Friday afternoon. They had one purpose in mind—to return to the sepulcher and embalm the body of the Lord. Just how early they started out on their journey nobody knows.

However, Luke tells us that it was "very early" (Luke 24:1); John says that they got there "when it was yet dark" (John 20:1); and Matthew says that it was "as it began to dawn toward the first day of the week" (Matthew 28:1). Evidently it was just before sunrise.

In their trembling hands the women carried the spices which they had begun to prepare before the Sabbath. They hoped that they might be able to persuade the guard to let them go into the tomb and embalm the body. Yet now, as they walked along the dark highway, a new worry troubled them. They remembered the stone which Joseph and Nicodemus had rolled in front of the sepulcher, a "very great" stone, much too heavy for women to move. "And they said among themselves, Who shall roll us away the stone from the door of the sepulchre?" Mark 16:3.

Now they are picking their way over the rough land near the place of burial. Suddenly they stop. There is the tomb, just ahead of them. But where is the stone? It is on one side; it has been rolled away!

They can hardly believe their eyes. What can this mean? Has someone been here already and robbed the tomb of its precious body? And what of the guard? What of the Roman seal on the tomb?

They can see no soldiers. As for the seal, it is broken. Who has dared to break this seal without permission from Pilate?

Suddenly they see an angel in human form sitting on that very stone, as though daring all Rome to do its worst. His face shines "like lightning," and his raiment is "white as snow."

Terrified, the women turn to flee from the scene, but they are halted by the angel's lovely voice. "Fear not ye," he says: "for I know that ye seek Jesus, which was crucified. He is not here: for He is risen, as He said. Come, see the place where the Lord lay." Matthew 28:5, 6.

At this they enter the sepulcher and find it empty, save for another beautiful angel sitting there. The body of Jesus is nowhere to be seen. As they look around, searching for it, the angel says, "Why seek ye the living among the dead? He is not here, but is risen: remember how He spake unto you when He was yet in Galilee, saying, The Son of man must be delivered into the hands of sinful men, and be crucified, and the third day rise again." Luke 24:5-7.

"Go your way," the angel continues, "tell His disciples and Peter that He goeth before you into Galilee: there shall ye see Him, as He said unto you." Mark 16:7.

At this the women—all but one—hurry from the sepul-

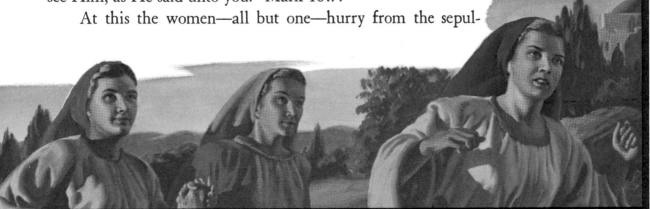

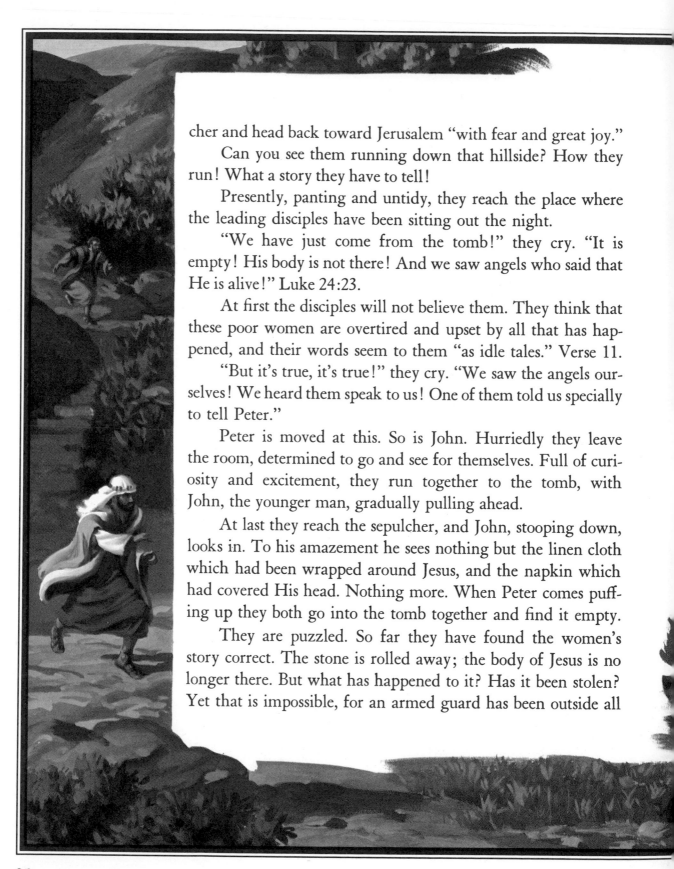

cher and head back toward Jerusalem "with fear and great joy."

Can you see them running down that hillside? How they run! What a story they have to tell!

Presently, panting and untidy, they reach the place where the leading disciples have been sitting out the night.

"We have just come from the tomb!" they cry. "It is empty! His body is not there! And we saw angels who said that He is alive!" Luke 24:23.

At first the disciples will not believe them. They think that these poor women are overtired and upset by all that has happened, and their words seem to them "as idle tales." Verse 11.

"But it's true, it's true!" they cry. "We saw the angels ourselves! We heard them speak to us! One of them told us specially to tell Peter."

Peter is moved at this. So is John. Hurriedly they leave the room, determined to go and see for themselves. Full of curiosity and excitement, they run together to the tomb, with John, the younger man, gradually pulling ahead.

At last they reach the sepulcher, and John, stooping down, looks in. To his amazement he sees nothing but the linen cloth which had been wrapped around Jesus, and the napkin which had covered His head. Nothing more. When Peter comes puffing up they both go into the tomb together and find it empty.

They are puzzled. So far they have found the women's story correct. The stone is rolled away; the body of Jesus is no longer there. But what has happened to it? Has it been stolen? Yet that is impossible, for an armed guard has been outside all night. Can it be that Jesus has risen from the dead? Can it be that He is indeed alive?

They hurry back to the city to tell the others what they have found. Only Mary Magdalene lingers by the empty tomb. Alone, she stoops down and looks into the sepulcher. There she sees "two angels in white sitting, the one at the head, and the other at the feet, where the body of Jesus had lain."

They say to her, "Woman, why weepest thou?"

She says, "Because they have taken away my Lord, and I know not where they have laid Him."

Just then Mary looks around and sees someone standing near her. Supposing him to be the gardener, she says, "Sir, if thou have borne Him hence, tell me where thou hast laid Him, and I will take Him away."

Then the gardener speaks—God's Gardener. He says but one word: "Mary." But it is enough. She recognizes Him immediately.

"Master!" she says, running toward Him.

"Touch Me not," He says; "for I am not yet ascended to My Father: but go to My brethren, and say unto them, I ascend unto My Father, and your Father; and to My God, and your God." John 20:17.

Then He is gone. But Mary knows now that the story of the angels is true. She has seen Him herself! She has heard His voice! He is alive! He is risen from the dead!

Though full of weariness from the long night vigil, with wildly beating heart she rushes headlong to the city to tell the others the wonderful news. The sun is rising over the Jordan Valley, bathing all the mountains round about Jerusalem with the light of a new day.

Another sun is shining too, for Jesus is risen, the Sun of Righteousness, whose golden rays shall shine on all the earth through all the years to come. The darkness of the tomb has yielded to the morning light of eternal redemption.

Twin sunrise! Glorious dawn of a great new day for the children of men!

The Last Good-by

FOR forty days after His death on Calvary, Jesus met with His disciples. Precious days!

True, He was not with them all the time, but they felt He was very near to them, likely to appear among them any minute; and it was always so good to see Him when He came.

After He had met with the seven fishermen by the lakeside, and invited them to breakfast, news of it spread all over Galilee. Hundreds of people who knew Jesus wanted to see Him again.

Many of them had not been able to go to Jerusalem for the Passover, and they were eager to know what had happened there. Rumors had reached them that Jesus had been arrested and crucified, and then had risen from the dead. Could it all be true?

From far and near they began to move toward one central meeting place—"a mountain," the Bible says—perhaps where Jesus had met with them so many times before. Soon there were more than five hundred present, all talking eagerly about the great events of the past few weeks, and all wondering whether Jesus would appear to them now.

Some thought that, seeing He was risen from the dead, He might reveal His power in a very wonderful way and set up the kingdom of Israel again, with Himself as King. They were sure He would appear among them in a blaze of light and glory. Then suddenly someone caught sight of a familiar figure walking there on the mountainside, just as Jesus had come among them so many times in the dear old days they remembered so well.

At once the cry went up, "It is the Lord; it is the Lord!" All five hundred saw Him at once, so that there could never be any question about His having risen from the dead.

Now it is that He says to them, "All power is given unto Me in heaven and in earth. Go ye therefore, and teach all nations, baptizing them in the name of the Father, and of the Son, and of the Holy Ghost: teaching them to observe all things whatsoever I have commanded you: and, lo, I am with you alway, even unto the end of the world."

This, then, is what He wants them to do. Not to stay around Galilee, working at their old jobs, but to go everywhere

telling others of the beautiful things He has taught them. How good it is to know that, though He has "all power . . . in heaven and in earth," He will never forget them! Never! He will be one with them in all their joys and sorrows "even unto the end of the world." They are never to feel alone. Always He will be thinking of them in love.

Something Jesus says at this time leads the eleven apostles to return to Jerusalem. At any rate, that is where we find them next in the Bible story, and here Jesus meets with them once more, "Eating together with them." Acts 1:4, margin. Now it is that He promises to give them power to preach and teach His message, saying, "And ye shall be witnesses unto Me both in Jerusalem, and in all Judaea, and in Samaria, and unto the uttermost part of the earth."

This is a new idea. Fancy a group of poor, humble fisher-folk like them witnessing in Jerusalem, of all places, where the priests and Pharisees live! And how can they, with no money and no possessions, ever go to the uttermost part of the earth?

Still wondering what Jesus can mean, they walk with Him to Bethany, a little way out of Jerusalem. This is where Mary and Martha live, and where Lazarus was raised from the dead only a few weeks before.

Now Jesus is looking at His disciples with a special tenderness. The hour of parting is at hand. He knows that He must soon leave them and return to heaven.

There is sadness in His heart. He loves these dear men, every one of them. He has lived with them for more than three years. He knows all about them; how much they have given up for Him, and how much they soon must suffer for His sake.

Dear Peter! Dear James! Dear, dear John! And Thomas, too, bless him, despite his doubts. And Matthew, Philip, and all the rest. Such good men and true, with all their faults!

"Bless you, bless you, every one!" He says, and there are tears in His voice, I think.

Suddenly they notice that He is rising into the air. He is going away! Yes! Up, up, up He goes, farther and farther, until at last a cloud receives Him out of their sight.

He has gone, but still they look, their eyes peering into the depths of space, hoping against hope that they may catch one more glimpse of Him. But He is gone, gone! And the dreadful feeling comes over them that He is gone for good. For a moment a desperate sadness fills their hearts.

Then all of a sudden they notice two strangers standing near them, both dressed in white. Who can they be?

"Ye men of Galilee," say the strangers, "why stand ye gazing up into heaven? this same Jesus, which is taken up from

you into heaven, shall so come in like manner as ye have seen Him go into heaven."

Now they know! Surely these two men are really angels, sent by their beloved Master to comfort their hearts with the promise that someday He will come back again.

How kind, how thoughtful of Him! On His way to the glory land, with all the shining host of heaven around Him, He has remembered His friends left behind on earth!

And they "returned to Jerusalem with great joy."

All sadness gone, they are "continually in the temple, praising and blessing God." Had not the angels said He would return? And that it would be "this same Jesus" who would come back, not another?

Beautiful, blessed hope! "This same Jesus" is to come again. The very same Jesus who healed the sick, raised the dead, loved the children, and told such beautiful stories—He is coming again. The same dear Jesus of Nazareth, Capernaum, and Cana, who did so many kind deeds for the poor and needy, who was always so gentle and gracious and good—He is coming again.

It will not be another Jesus, a different Jesus, but "this same Jesus." Time will not age or alter Him, for He is "the same yesterday, and to day, and for ever." When He comes back down that shining pathway through the skies, it will be the same Jesus who went away, unchanged by the changing years. We shall know Him by the smile on His face, by the sweet melody of His voice, and by the marks of the nails in His hands.

Lessons Jesus Taught

He Taught Love does not complete E. G. White's explanation of Christ's parables. She focuses her remarkable spiritual sensitivity on many more parables in *Lessons Jesus Taught*. Once again you can have the illuminating experience of finding new meaning in stories that were meant to help us understand God and His plan for the world. Discover what Jesus meant when He talked about wedding clothes, a pearl of great price, and a fig tree.

He Taught Love

The closer we look at the parables, the clearer we picture our relationship to the heavenly Father. Discover the message Jesus had for us when He told the parables of the mustard seed and the wise embezzler. This book selects 12 chapters from *Lessons Jesus Taught* (see above). Even if you have all the parables memorized, you will find eye-opening concepts and new reservoirs of inspiration in every chapter. Softcover.

Eight Steps to Health and Happiness

Reveals the basics of strengthening the body and recovering from disease. Each of the eight steps is grounded in common sense. You might wonder why you haven't thought of them before. Softcover.

Quick and Easy Cooking

This book gives you 104 recipes already arranged into menus to save you time in planning balanced, nutritious meals. They are quick to prepare, usually taking less than 50 minutes from the time you walk into the kitchen until you call everyone to the table. Best of all, these low-fat recipes fight cancer while preserving your cardiovascular system for a long and happy life. You will be surprised at how easy it is to eat healthfully and enjoy it. Softcover.

For more information on these books, mail the postpaid card or write:

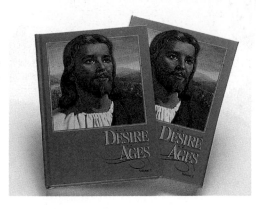